EARLY PEOPLES

AUSTRALIAN ABORIGINES

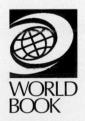

WORLD
BOOK

World Book
a Scott Fetzer company
Chicago
www.worldbookonline.com

22.44

j994
Australian

World Book, Inc.
233 N. Michigan Avenue
Chicago, IL 60601
U.S.A.

For information about other World Book publications, visit
our Web site at http://www.worldbookonline.com or call
1-800-WORLDBK (967-5325).
For information about sales to schools and libraries, call
1-800-975-3250 (United States), or 1-800-837-5365 (Canada).

Library of Congress Cataloging-in-Publication Data
Australian aborigines.
    p. cm. -- (Early peoples)
  Includes index.
    Summary: "A discussion of the early Aborigines, including who the
people were, where they lived, the rise of civilization, social structure,
religion, art and architecture, science and technology, daily life, and
entertainment and sports. Features include timelines, fact boxes, glossary,
list of recommended reading and web sites, and index"--Provided by
publisher.
  ISBN 978-0-7166-2128-7
  1. Aboriginal Australians--Juvenile literature. I. World Book, Inc.
DU123.4.A87 2009
994.01--dc22
                            2008032223

Printed in China
1 2 3 4 5 13 12 11 10 09

STAFF

EXECUTIVE COMMITTEE
President
  Paul A. Gazzolo
Vice President and Chief Marketing
Officer
  Patricia Ginnis
Vice President and Chief Financial Officer
  Donald D. Keller
Vice President and Editor in Chief
  Paul A. Kobasa
Director, Human Resources
  Bev Ecker
Chief Technology Officer
  Tim Hardy
Managing Director, International
  Benjamin Hinton

EDITORIAL
Editor in Chief
  Paul A. Kobasa
Associate Director, Supplementary
Publications
  Scott Thomas
Managing Editor, Supplementary
Publications
  Barbara A. Mayes
Senior Editor, Supplementary Publications
  Kristina Vaicikonis
Manager, Research, Supplementary
Publications
  Cheryl Graham
Manager, Contracts & Compliance
  (Rights & Permissions)
  Loranne K. Shields

Administrative Assistant
  Ethel Matthews
Editors
  Nicholas Kilzer
  Scott Richardson
  Christine Sullivan

GRAPHICS AND DESIGN
Associate Director
  Sandra M. Dyrlund
Manager
  Tom Evans
Coordinator, Design Development
and Production
  Brenda B. Tropinski

EDITORIAL ADMINISTRATION
Director, Systems and Projects
  Tony Tills
Senior Manager, Publishing Operations
  Timothy Falk

PRODUCTION
Director, Manufacturing and Pre-Press
  Carma Fazio
Manufacturing Manager
  Steve Hueppchen
Production/Technology Manager
  Anne Fritzinger
Production Specialist
  Curley Hunter
Proofreader
  Emilie Schrage

MARKETING
Chief Marketing Officer
  Patricia Ginnis
Associate Director, School and Library
Marketing
  Jennifer Parello

Produced for World Book by
 White-Thomson Publishing Ltd.
+44 (0)845 362 8240
www.wtpub.co.uk
Steve White-Thomson, President

Writer: John Haywood
Editors: Valerie Weber, Robert Famighetti
Designer: Clare Nicholas
Photo Researcher: Amy Sparks
Map Artist: Stefan Chabluk
Illustrator: Adam Hook (p. 48)
Fact Checker: Charlene Rimsa
Proofreader: Catherine Gardner
Indexer: Nila Glikin

Consultant:
Tim Rowse
Senior Fellow, History Program
Research School of Social Sciences
The Australian National University

TABLE OF CONTENTS

Glossary There is a glossary on pages 60-61. Terms defined in the glossary are in type **that looks like this** on their first appearance on any spread (two facing pages).

Additional Resources Books for further reading and recommended Web sites are listed on page 62. Because of the nature of the Internet, some Web site addresses may have changed since publication. The publisher has no responsibility for any such changes or for the content of cited sources.

WHO WERE THE ABORIGINES?

The Aborigines *(ab uh RIHJ uh neez)* were the first people to live in Australia. Their ancestors arrived in Australia more than 50,000 years ago. Until European settlers arrived in Australia in 1788, the Aborigines were the only people to live on the continent. Scientists estimate that from 500,000 to 1 million Aborigines lived in Australia when Europeans landed there.

The Aborigines hunted wild animals, fished, and gathered wild plants for food. They were **nomadic**, moving with the seasons to look for new sources of food. The Aborigines rarely built permanent homes because they usually did not stay in one place for very long. They had few possessions. They made tools of stone, bone, and wood. Metals and pottery were unknown to the Aborigines. Most of Australia has a warm climate, so for most of the year, the Aborigines did not wear clothes.

▼ About one-third of Australia is desert. Most of the desert, such as the area surrounding Kata Tjuta *(KAT uh JOOT uh)*, a group of giant rock formations also known as the Olgas (below), supports only scattered clumps of grass and very few bushes and trees. Aborigines were skilled at surviving in such a harsh environment.

▲ Water lily pads grow in a **billabong** *(BIHL uh bong)* in northwestern Australia. Billabongs are shallow lakes left behind when a river changes course. They are rich in fish, water birds, and edible plants. The roots and seeds of water lilies were important foods for the Aborigines. The word *billabong* is an Aboriginal word meaning *dead river* that has entered into common usage in Australia.

The Aborigines were divided into hundreds of tribes. Each tribe had its own territory without rulers or governments. The tribal **elders** met to make important decisions. The elders were older men who were respected for their knowledge and wisdom. The Aborigines did not write. All of their knowledge was passed from generation to generation by word of mouth through stories and songs or by paintings on rocks. The Aborigines believed that all living things were connected to an ancient time called the **Dreamtime**. The Dreamtime was a period when powerful spirit beings shaped the world and created the first people, animals, and plants.

WHAT IS IN A NAME?

The word *Aborigine* comes from the Latin words *ab origine*, which mean *from the beginning*. European explorers gave the name to the people they encountered upon landing in Australia. When spelled with a small *a*, the word *aborigines* refers to any people whose ancestors were the first people to live in a place or region.

WHERE DID THE ABORIGINES LIVE?

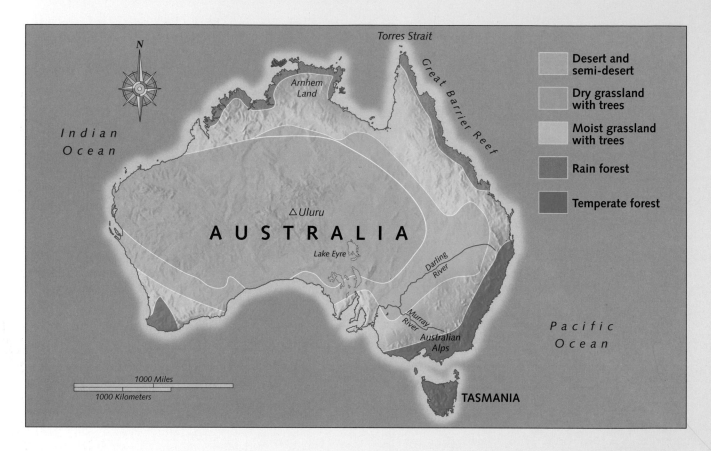

	Desert and semi-desert
	Dry grassland with trees
	Moist grassland with trees
	Rain forest
	Temperate forest

Australia is the smallest of the seven continents on Earth. But it is still a huge territory of almost 3 million square miles (7.7 million square kilometers), and it has several types of environments. Aborigines lived in every part of Australia, following many different ways of life adapted to the conditions of the local environment.

The most favorable area for Aboriginal settlement was the southeast coast. This was the most **fertile** area of Australia. Year-round rainfall supported forests with plentiful plant foods and game animals to hunt. There were also good opportunities for fishing, gathering shellfish, and hunting seals on the coast. In most parts of

▲ Australia has a number of natural environments. Deserts and grasslands with scattered trees cover most of the continent.

Australia, rain falls only during certain seasons of the year. In the tropical north, most rain falls in the summer (December to March in Australia), while in the southwest it falls mainly in the winter (June to September). In many areas where rainfall is seasonal, the environment is dominated by grassland dotted with bushes and trees. Aborigines in these areas preferred to live near rivers and water holes, where animals and plants were most plentiful. Food was often scarce in the dry seasons. The center of Australia receives very little rain and is mostly desert. Deserts support

MAKING FIRE

Aborigines usually made fires by rubbing a sharp-edged piece of hard wood across a piece of soft, dry mulga wood. Once the mulga became red-hot, it was used to light kindling made of dried kangaroo **dung**. Dried grass was added to the kindling. The Aborigines blew gently on the smoldering dung, causing the grass to burst into flame. Making fire this way is hard work. Aborigines liked to carry smoldering firesticks with them, so that they could light fires quickly whenever they wanted.

few plants and animals, but Aborigines learned how to survive even in these harsh places.

The Australian environment has changed considerably since the Aborigines first arrived over 50,000 years ago. At that time, Australia had a cooler and wetter climate, and there were more rivers, lakes, and forests. About 11,500 years ago, the climate became hotter and drier, causing deserts to spread and some lakes and rivers to dry up.

Changing the Environment

The Aborigines also changed the Australian environment by lighting bush fires. Burning undergrowth and dead grass encouraged the growth of new grass shoots. Grazing animals that the Aborigines liked to hunt, such as gray kangaroos and **wallabies** (a **species**, or type, of small kangaroo), benefited from this. It was, however, bad for animals that mostly ate tree leaves. These animals included many species of giant **marsupials** *(mahr SOO pee uhlz)*. These **megafauna** *(meh guh FAW nuh)*, or large animals, included a giant kangaroo called Procoptodon *(proh KOP tuh don)* that grew to nearly 10 feet (3 meters) tall. Years of burning created a more open landscape with fewer trees and less food for the megafauna, which became **extinct** about 20,000 years ago.

This practice of deliberate burning was called **firestick** farming after the slow-burning sticks Aborigines used to light the fires. Firestick farming was not really farming, however. The Aborigines never became farmers, perhaps because Australia has few native species of plants that are suitable for cultivation or animals suitable to raise as livestock.

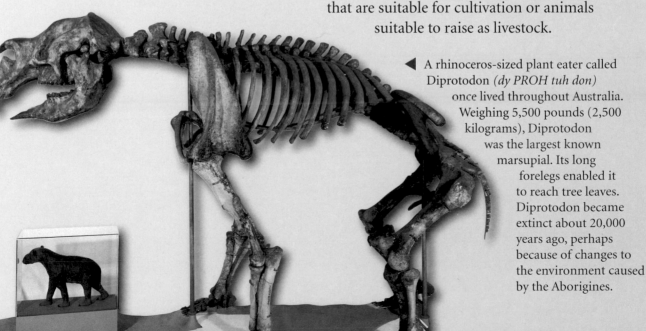

◄ A rhinoceros-sized plant eater called Diprotodon *(dy PROH tuh don)* once lived throughout Australia. Weighing 5,500 pounds (2,500 kilograms), Diprotodon was the largest known marsupial. Its long forelegs enabled it to reach tree leaves. Diprotodon became extinct about 20,000 years ago, perhaps because of changes to the environment caused by the Aborigines.

HOW DO WE KNOW ABOUT THE ABORIGINES' HISTORY?

The Aborigines never used writing to record their history. Most of what we know about Aboriginal history comes from the science of **archaeology** *(ar kee AH luh jee)*. Archaeology is the study of the material remains, such as buildings, tools, burial sites, and even garbage, left by people who lived in the past. **Archaeologists** discover these remains by **excavating** *(EHKS kuh vayt ing)* sites where people once lived and worked.

Finding Aboriginal sites is not easy. The Aborigines lived lightly on the land and did not build homes from long-lasting materials. Most Aboriginal homes were simple huts built of branches and tree bark. They were not intended to be used for long, and they soon fell down and rotted away to nothing. Many of the

▶ Fossilized human footprints discovered by archaeologists at Willandra Lakes, in southeastern Australia, are from 19,000 to 23,000 years old. Early Aborigines made the footprints when walking across a muddy lake bed. The footprints were preserved when they were buried by blown sand after the lake dried up.

REST IN PEACE

Until recently, archaeologists had little respect for remains they found in Aboriginal burial places. They dug up skeletons for study and then stored them in museums. No one bothered to ask the Aborigines what they thought about this. Modern Aborigines have campaigned successfully to have their ancestors' remains returned to them for reburial, and archaeologists have changed the way they study burial sites.

Aborigines' possessions were made of wood and vegetable fibers. Once they had been thrown away, they also quickly disappeared. A few discarded stone tools are often the only traces of an Aboriginal campsite.

Archaeologists search for sites in places that they believe would have been attractive to Aborigines. These places include riverbanks, seashores, and desert water holes. Archaeologists also search for sites under overhanging cliffs. Aborigines often camped in these natural shelters.

Besides art and other markings left on rock faces, the most obvious Aboriginal sites are **shell mounds** along Australia's coasts. These mounds are basically garbage dumps. Aborigines visited favorite sites time and time again. Over hundreds of years, huge mounds of discarded shells, animal bones, and ash built up. Some mounds are up to 30 feet (9 meters) tall. Studying these sites tells us what Aborigines ate and how they moved between campsites as the seasons changed.

Talking to People

In remote areas of Australia, some Aborigines were able to live according to their traditional ways well into the 1900's. **Anthropologists** (AN thruh POL uh jihstz)—people who study human beings—studied these Aborigines. They talked to the Aborigines about their lives and recorded their customs and beliefs. Early European explorers also wrote descriptions of Aboriginal life. These writings often show a lack of respect for and understanding of the Aborigines' way of life.

▲ An Aboriginal rock painting discovered at Faraway Bay, in the modern state of Western Australia, may be more than 20,000 years old. Archaeologists estimate that the many markings, paintings, and drawings at Faraway Bay rank among the oldest known artworks in the world.

ORIGINS OF THE ABORIGINES

The ancestors of the Aborigines lived in Asia. About 60,000 years ago, groups of people began to move east, following the coast of the Indian Ocean. They reached what is now Indonesia a short time later. Sometime before 50,000 years ago, they began to settle in Australia.

This journey was possible because it took place during the most recent **ice age**, when ice sheets covered large areas of the Northern Hemisphere as well as large areas around Antarctica. During ice ages, oceans grow smaller because more water is locked up in ice. At the height of the last ice age, so much water was frozen in ice sheets that the sea levels were at least 330 feet (100 meters) lower than they are now. As a result, dry land linked many places that are now separated by water. Today, Indonesia is a chain of islands. But 50,000 years ago, the islands were highlands above a forested plain. Scientists believe the ancestors of the Aborigines probably could have walked from mainland Asia to Indonesia.

Australia and Indonesia were not connected by a land bridge because the ocean between them was too deep, even during the last ice age. The Aborigines could only have reached Australia in boats or rafts that were strong enough to sail long distances. **Archaeologists** think that the Aborigines' boats may have been made of bamboo. Bamboo is light, floats well, and is waterproof. Indonesians still use it to make rafts.

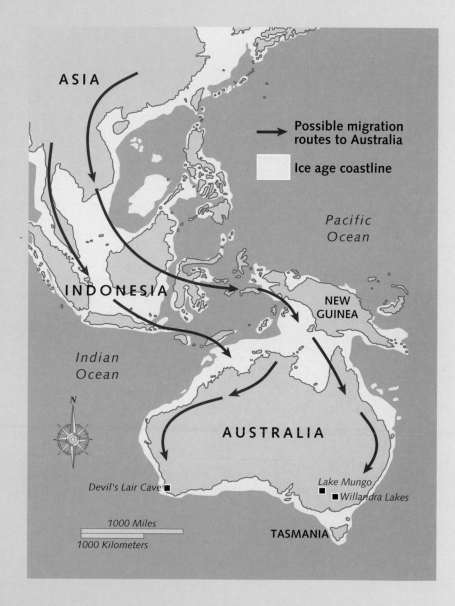

Possible migration routes to Australia

Ice age coastline

ASIA

Pacific Ocean

INDONESIA

NEW GUINEA

Indian Ocean

N

AUSTRALIA

Devil's Lair Cave

Lake Mungo
Willandra Lakes

1000 Miles
1000 Kilometers

TASMANIA

▲ The ancestors of the Aborigines migrated from Asia to Indonesia over a land bridge that existed during the last ice age. Archaeologists believe these people used boats or rafts to reach Australia.

ICE AGES

There have been many ice ages during Earth's history—periods when ice sheets covered vast regions of land. The most recent ice age, the Pleistocene Epoch *(PLYS tuh seen EHP uhk)*, began 2 million years ago and ended about 11,500 years ago. During that period, some glaciers were as much as 10,000 feet (3,000 meters) thick.

The Discovery of Australia

Today, 200 miles (320 kilometers) of open sea separates Australia from Indonesia. Scientists estimate that during the last ice age, the distance was only about 100 miles (160 kilometers) because of lower sea levels. Archaeologists are unsure how the Aborigines discovered Australia. Some experts believe they may have set out from Indonesia on a voyage to find new lands. Others believe they discovered Australia by accident after being blown off course when sailing along the Indonesian coast.

◀ Bamboo is a tall, fast-growing **species** of grass that is native to Southeast Asia. Its shiny woody stems are strong, flexible, lightweight, and water-proof. Depending on their thickness and length, bamboo stems are used today to make houses, scaffolding, pipes, furniture, baskets, and musical instruments. Experts think that the Aborigines may have reached Australia using boats or rafts made of bamboo.

ABORIGINES SETTLE AUSTRALIA

Scientists do not know exactly when or where the Aborigines first landed in Australia. **Archaeologists** believe that the Aborigines probably arrived in northwestern Australia. This part of the Australian continent is closest to Indonesia. However, sea levels rose as ice sheets melted at the end of the last **ice age**. As a result, the places where the Aborigines probably arrived were flooded and now lie under the sea. The oldest archaeological sites discovered in Australia are actually in the south.

It is possible that several waves of settlers arrived over many years. However, some archaeologists speculate that only a small number of people, perhaps only a few hundred, reached Australia. The early Aborigines would have found Australia a good place to live. The climate was cooler and wetter than it is today. Plant and animal life was more plentiful because of the higher rainfall.

Archaeological sites in the Willandra Lakes region show that the Aborigines had reached southeastern Australia by at least 45,000 years ago. Scientists estimate that Aborigines lived at Devil's Lair Cave in southwestern Australia

◀ An eroded sand dune, known as the Walls of China, marks the eastern edge of Lake Mungo, a dried-up lake bed where archaeologists found the continent's oldest dated human remains. Aborigines lived around the lake for thousands of years, until the water disappeared about 14,000 years ago. The lake is now part of the Willandra Lakes World Heritage Area.

nearly 40,000 years ago. These sites are all more than 2,000 miles (3,200 kilometers) from the northwestern coast of Australia. Archaeologists believe that the Aborigines needed time to adapt to life in Australia and that they spread slowly over the land. If Aborigines lived in southern Australia 45,000 years ago, their ancestors must have arrived in the northwest much earlier than that.

Icy Tasmania

The Australian island of Tasmania lies off the southern tip of the continent. During the last ice age, the island was part of the Australian mainland. Archaeological **excavations** in several caves have shown that Aborigines lived in Tasmania more than 30,000 years ago. Tasmania was the southern-most place in the world to be inhabited by people during the last ice age.

LAKE MUNGO

The oldest human remains found in Australia are parts of a male skeleton from a burial site at Lake Mungo in the present-day state of New South Wales. Archaeologists believe this skeleton may be about 40,000 years old. During the last Ice age, the lake's fresh water, which would have attracted wildlife, made it an ideal place for Aborigines to live. Today, Mungo is a dry lake bed.

▼ At Kow Swamp in the modern state of Victoria, archaeologists found an ancient Aboriginal burial site. The remains, which included a skull, are believed to be from 9,000 to 13,500 years old. The skull is much longer than normal. Archaeologists think that changing the shape of the skull—perhaps by binding the head tightly during infancy—may have been a cultural practice among early Aborigines. The skull was returned to local Aborigines for reburial in 1992.

LIMITED CONTACT

Rising sea levels at the end of the last **ice age** made Australia harder to reach. It was never totally isolated from the rest of the world, however. The Aborigines occasionally made contact with the peoples of New Guinea and Indonesia to the north. New types of fishing gear and new methods of boatbuilding reached Australia in this way.

One of the most important results of these contacts was the introduction of the **dingo** about 3,500 years ago. Dingoes are wild dogs closely related to the wild dogs of India and Southeast Asia. Experts believe that seafarers from Indonesia or Southeast Asia brought dingoes to Australia. The Aborigines kept dingoes as hunting dogs and watchdogs. They also slept with the dogs to keep warm on cold nights.

Wild dingoes live in packs and hunt kangaroos and **wallabies**. Native **marsupial carnivores** (meat-eaters) became **extinct** after dingoes arrived. The marsupials were less efficient hunters than the dingoes and could not compete with them for food. Marsupial predators survived until the 1900's on Tasmania, because the land became an island before wild dingoes reached it.

▼ Dingoes, a breed of wild dog that originated in India or Southeast Asia, served the Aborigines as hunting dogs. After dingoes were introduced to Australia around 3,500 years ago, some **species** of native carnivores, such as the Tasmanian tiger, a wolf-like marsupial with striped fur, became extinct because they were less efficient hunters.

AUSTRALIA'S FIRST EXPORT
The Makassans went to Australia to catch worm-like marine animals called sea cucumbers. The dried bodies of sea cucumbers are known as trepang *(trih PANG)*. Soup made from dried trepang was popular in China because it was believed to cure several illnesses.

Makassan Influence

During the 1600's, merchants from the city of Makassar *(muh KAS uhr)* on the Indonesian island of Sulawesi *(soo luh WAY see)* began making yearly voyages to Arnhem Land, a region in northwestern Australia.

The Makassans strongly influenced the Aboriginal Yolngu *(YOLN yoo)* people of Arnhem Land. The Yolngu adopted dozens of Makassan words into their language. Some Aboriginal men became sailors on Makassan ships and traveled to Indonesia. The Makassans did not settle permanently in Australia, but some Makassan sailors lived with Aboriginal women

▲ The Makassan traders used a type of sailing ship called a proa *(PROH uh)* to sail between Indonesia and Australia. The traders' proas generally had one mast and were about 60 feet (20 meters) long. They had narrow hulls to make them fast. Their speed made proas popular with pirates as well as traders.

and had children with them. Many modern Yolngu are partly descended from Indonesians. The Yolngu also acquired pipes and tobacco, pottery, dugout canoes, and iron knives from the Makassans but never started making things from metal themselves. The Makassans are thought to have accidentally introduced smallpox to Australia. This disease killed many Aborigines.

TRIBES, CLANS, AND TERRITORIES

The prehistoric Aborigines were divided into about 600 different tribes who spoke around 300 different languages. Each tribe had from a few hundred up to about 2,000 members. Tribes were united by a common language and shared religious beliefs. Whole tribes were rarely together, however.

Tribes were divided into groups of about 50 people called **clans.** Each clan had its own territory. Most members of a clan were closely related to one another by birth or marriage. Clan members were also united by the belief that they shared a common spirit ancestor in the **Dreamtime**, or Dreaming, the time of creation. People from one clan often married into another

clan, and people from different clans often cooperated with one another in daily tasks of survival.

Aboriginal clans were not ruled by chiefs or kings, and they had no formal governments. Given their way of life, the prehistoric Aborigines did not need rulers to direct such important activities as obtaining food and conducting ceremonies. The Aborigines had laws, in the sense of shared and enforced ideas about right and wrong ways to act, but they had neither police nor judges. The Aborigines respected age, ability, and experience. The tribal elders met to make important decisions and deal with troublemakers. Everyone had the responsibility of working for the good of the

A tribal **elder** of the Ngarrindjeri *(NAHR rihn jehr ee)* people of southeastern Australia wears paint and hair ornaments in preparation for a ceremony marking the return of Aboriginal remains that were removed from their graves about 100 years ago. Aboriginal elders traditionally have been the older, more experienced members of a clan.

▶ An Aborigine spearfishing in the traditional manner, while another man looks on. An Aboriginal clan would often allow people from another clan facing starvation to enter its territory to gather food. But if one clan entered another's territory to hunt or fish without permission, the result could be a war.

whole group. Modern Aborigines retain many of the traditional values of their ancestors.

Prominent landmarks and such natural barriers as rivers marked the borders of a clan's territory. Each person had a deep spiritual relationship with his or her territory. If food was scarce, a clan could ask for permission to hunt on another clan's territory. Clans usually gave their permission. A clan may have shared its territory because its members had relatives in the other clan. Perhaps, the clan knew that someday it might need the same favor.

Warfare

Hunting without permission on another clan's territory was a serious offense. Trespassers risked being attacked. If a trespasser's relatives wanted revenge against the attackers, a war could break out. Tribes did not usually fight wars to conquer other tribes or drive them out of their territories. However, tribes sometimes went to war to gain access to food or other resources, and these wars could be vicious. Women and children were often killed along with the men. Wars usually ended with a meeting between tribal elders or a festival.

MESSAGE STICKS

Aborginal clans and tribes sometimes communicated using message sticks. These sticks were solid pieces of wood from 8 to 10 inches (20 to 25 centimeters) long that were carved with lines that symbolized people engaged in different activities. The sticks were used to declare war as well as to invite another clan or tribe to a festival or other gathering. Messengers delivered the sticks, sometimes over long distances. The messengers also memorized a verbal message.

THE FAMILY

The extended family was the most important unit in Aboriginal society. A typical family might consist of a man, his wives, and their children, and sometimes an aunt, an uncle, or grandparents. Aboriginal men usually married when they were in their late 20's or early 30's. Girls married when they were in their early teens. When a man was about 50 years old, he took a second wife, who was usually in her teens.

Marriages could unite a man and woman from the same **clan** or from different clans. In either case, a marriage was viewed by Aborigines as a relationship between families, not just between individuals.

Men and women had separate roles in Aboriginal society. Men hunted and made tools. Women collected and prepared plants for food, looked after the children, and carried everything when the family moved camp. Men and women also had different roles to play in festivals and religious ceremonies.

▲ An Aborigine family rests in the shade of a simple shelter built of dry grass, in an 1848 engraving showing a camp in Portland Bay, in southwestern Australia. The real center of an Aboriginal home was the campfire, which was kept burning night and day.

Men considered women's roles in daily life and in ceremonies to be inferior. Generally, older women commanded much greater respect than younger women and girls.

Aborigine families often did not have many children. Aborigines had to move camp often, so women tried to wait until their youngest child was old enough to walk before having another baby. That way, they would never have to carry more than one child. Many children died of natural causes. The Aborigines also knew that if their clans grew large, there might not be enough food for everyone. If food was in short supply, the Aborigines might kill some babies. They believed this was necessary to make sure that other members of the group did not go hungry.

An Aboriginal Home

Aborigines did not usually bother to build permanent homes. In warm weather, parents and young children slept together outside around a campfire. If they needed shelter from the wind and rain, they built a simple round hut by laying tree bark over a framework of wooden sticks. Older children and grandparents had their own huts.

Old Age

When people became too old to find food on their own, their sons looked after them. Older people were respected. When food was scarce, however, the family let the older people go hungry. Aborigines believed they should not give food to someone who probably did not have long to live.

▼ Aborigines sit outside a hut made of dried grass and sticks, in an 1886 photograph. The European-style clothing worn by the Aborigines and their use of European cooking pots reflect the influence of Christian missionaries.

THE DREAMTIME

Like modern Aborigines, prehistoric Aborigines had a deep spiritual link to the land. The most important religious belief of all Australian Aborigines was the **Dreamtime**, or Dreaming. The Dreamtime was the age of creation when spirit beings called **Dreamings** shaped the land and laid down laws and customs.

Aborigines believed that before the Dreamtime, the world was shapeless. There were no plants, animals, or people. The Dreamtime began when the Dreamings took the forms of animals and people. These powerful beings traveled over the land, giving it shape and creating **sacred** (holy) places. The routes they took, called **songlines**, could stretch for hundreds of miles.

The Dreamings also created the first plants, animals, and human beings. They made human beings the guardians of the land. The spirit beings gave each tribe a territory to live in and laws to live by. After the work of creation was complete, the spirit ancestors merged with such landmarks as lakes or mountains and continued to have a powerful spiritual presence.

▼ **Uluru** (also known as Ayers Rock), in what is now the Northern Territory, lies almost at the exact center of Australia. Uluru is sacred to the Aboriginal peoples who live around it. They tell many stories about how the rock was created. According to one of these stories, Uluru was shaped and scarred by two serpent-shaped Dreamings who fought each other there.

▲ A rock painting in northwestern Australia shows an ancestral Dreamtime spirit.

WHEN WAS THE DREAMTIME?

It is not possible to say when the Dreamtime was. According to Aboriginal belief, the Dreamtime could be visited during religious ceremonies. In this way, it is always the Dreamtime.

The Waugal

There were many different stories about the Dreamtime. The Noongar people of southwestern Australia believed that their land had been shaped by a snake-like Dreaming called the Waugal *(WOG uhl)*. As he slithered over the land, the Waugal created winding rivers and sand dunes. When he stopped to rest, the weight of the Waugal's body created lakes and bays along the seacoast. His droppings became piles of rocks. When the Waugal moved, his scales fell off, and they became trees. Finally, the Waugal's body turned into a 600-mile- (965-kilometer-) long mountain ridge. But the Waugal's spirit lived on to guide and protect the tribe. Tribal **elders** were able to talk with him during religious ceremonies.

The Aborigines believed that human beings have spirits that live forever. The spirits were created in the Dreamtime. They believed that a spirit took on human form by entering a baby's body a few months before it was born. The spirit left the body after a person died, traveled to the Land of the Dead, and became young again.

ABORIGINAL ROCK ART

▲ Aborigines blew paint around their hands to make handprints on a cave wall in the Bungle Bungle Range in Western Australia. The long oval shape was probably made by blowing paint around a **coolamon** *(KOO luh mahn)*, a type of bowl. Underneath the handprints is an outline of a crocodile. Experts believe that people made handprints as a way of showing that they had attended a ceremony.

Aboriginal rock art consists of paintings and carvings on rocks, cliff faces, and cave walls. It is one of the oldest art forms in the world. Some aboriginal rock art may be up to 40,000 years old.

The Aborigines did not create art for decoration or enjoyment. Art nearly always had a religious meaning. Paintings and carvings marked **sacred** sites and carried secret information about the **Dreamtime**. To renew their spiritual power and to ensure that the information they contained was not lost, old paintings were repainted when necessary.

Different regions of Australia had different styles of painting. The most complex paintings were made in northwestern Australia. These paintings include large groups of human figures and animals. They also show Dreamtime spirits called Wandjinas *(wahnd JIHN uhz)* in ceremonial headdresses. Some paintings show the arrival of Europeans with their sailing ships and guns.

Making Paint

Aboriginal artists used only a few colors for their paints. They ground **ocher** *(OH kuhr)* to make a red **pigment** (colored powder). Yellow and brown pigments came from clay rich in **manganese** *(MANG guh neez)*, a hard, brittle metal. Artists made black pigments from powdered charcoal and white pigment from **kaolin** *(KAY uh lihn)*, a fine, white clay. They mixed the pigments with water to make paint. Using a piece of charcoal, artists began by drawing an outline of their picture. Then they painted it using their fingers or brushes made of feathers.

Artists also made patterns by spraying paint from their mouths around an object. When they removed the object, its outline could be seen on the rock. The most common patterns of this type were made using hands. **Archaeologists** think that the hand outlines may have been a way for people to show that they had taken part in a ceremony.

Aborigines made rock carvings by using a hard stone to chip a pattern into the rock face. The patterns often resemble animal tracks. They are most common in the eastern half of Australia.

▶ A cave painting found in what is now Kakadu National Park, in Australia's Northern Territory. Common subjects for rock art included Dreamtime spirits, **rituals,** and handprints.

X-RAY PAINTINGS OF KAKADU

When artists in Kakadu in northwestern Australia painted people, animals, and fish, they often showed the bones and internal organs. These are known as X-ray paintings after the modern machines used to take photographs of people's bones and internal organs. Aborigines learned about the internal organs of animals while butchering them.

MAGIC AND SORCERY

Aborigines strongly believed in the power of magic to help or harm people. The Aborigines believed that sorcerers had links with the spirit beings of the **Dreamtime**. Almost all sorcerers were men.

Aborigines believed that sorcerers had amazing powers. These powers made sorcerers respected as well as feared. They could see into the future, make themselves invisible, bring rain, and kill their enemies with spells. Some could see into people's bodies and cure diseases. To help them work their magic, they carried small bags of charms. Crystals, special bones, mother-of-pearl, and **australites** were the most common charms. Australites are small, button- or lens-shaped pieces of glass found in southern Australia. Known elsewhere as tektites, australites probably were formed by the impact of meteorites and shaped by rapid flight through the atmosphere.

▼ A petroglyph *(PEHT ruh glihf)*, or rock carving, in New South Wales. The Aborigines believed such petroglyphs were made by spirit beings during the Dreamtime. Sorcerers were thought to derive their powers from these spirit beings.

Making Rain

The most important use of magic was to bring rain to make plants grow and provide drinking water for both humans and animals. The Aborigines believed that a spirit called the Rainbow Snake controlled rain. The Rainbow Snake was friendly to human beings. He would bring rain if he was pleased by **rituals** or special ceremonies. Mother-of-pearl was often used in these rituals because it was linked with the Rainbow Snake and with water. Mother-of-pearl, which is also called nacre *(NAY kuhr)*, is a shiny substance produced by oysters and other shell-forming mollusks *(MOL uhskz)*. It is deposited on the inner surface of shells and helps protect the animals from **parasites** and other foreign objects.

In the Great Victoria Desert, sorcerers mixed powdered mother-of-pearl with fresh grass while singing to the Rainbow Snake. Then they spat in the direction from which they hoped the rain would come. They sometimes threw white feathers into the air to ask the Rainbow Snake to send clouds. In other rituals, a sorcerer would cut himself and allow his blood to drip on the ground like raindrops.

LOVE CHARMS
Young men and women often asked sorcerers to make someone fall in love with them. The sorcerer would prepare a love charm for them. In many parts of Australia, these charms were made of strands of red feathers from a parakeet, such as this crimson rosella.

Harmful Magic

Some sorcerers were believed to wear slippers made of feathers that made them invisible. These sorcerers could even change shape. It was also believed that they could kill enemies simply by pointing a magic bone at them and singing a secret song over it. Often, when people were told that they had been cursed in this way, they were so frightened that they soon died.

LAW AND ORDER

Aborigines lived by traditional laws given to them by the spirit beings in the **Dreamtime**. There were only a few types of crime in Aboriginal society. The main crimes included theft, violence, and breaking marriage laws. Another type of crime was breaking religious laws. For example, some areas of land were considered so **sacred** that most people could not go near them. Women and boys were forbidden to see certain symbols carved on wood or stones. People were severely punished for violating these religious laws. Theft was rare because the Aborigines had very few possessions.

The tribal **elders** decided what to do about people who broke the rules. Punishments depended on the seriousness of the crime. Someone who had committed a minor crime, such as theft, might simply be made fun of in public. This mockery showed the offender that everyone else thought his or her behavior was wrong. People who broke religious laws, such as not performing a **ritual** properly, were told that the spirit ancestors would punish them by causing them to have an accident or some other misfortune.

A RITUAL FIGHT

In Arnhem Land in northwestern Australia, people settled disputes by a ritual fight. The offender had to stand still while the victim's family threw blunt spears at him. Then he ran while they threw sharp spears at him. After the offender had been wounded or killed, the ritual ended with a dance.

▼ The 2006 Australian film *Ten Canoes* is a story of tribal law in Aboriginal Australia. After a man kills another man from a neighboring **clan,** the slain man's clan is allowed to retaliate—but only against the killer. In this way, justice is served and the clans avoid a war.

Violent Crime

Violent crimes were treated more seriously. If a victim or a victim's relatives took revenge on the offender, the violence could get out of control. This situation was dangerous for the whole group because other families could easily get drawn into the fighting to support their friends. The elders worked toward a peaceful end to disputes between families to stop this from happening. Aborigines did not believe that anyone could die by accident. A person who fell out of a tree or died of an illness might really have been murdered by harmful magic.

Sorcerers were asked to investigate mysterious deaths. They performed rituals that helped them identify the killer. The most common punishment for a serious offense was to be stabbed in the thigh with a spear. People who frequently behaved badly were expelled from the tribe or killed. Sometimes magic was used to kill a dangerous offender.

▶ Spears (foreground) and **woomeras** (spear-throwers) were used mainly for hunting, but Aboriginal weapons could be just as effective against people. Violent crimes and violent punishments sometimes occurred in Aboriginal Australia.

FESTIVALS AND CEREMONIES

Aborigines held many religious festivals and ceremonies. Some were held to show respect for the spirit beings and to encourage plants and animals to grow and increase in numbers. Others were held when children became adults or when people died. Festivals were also an opportunity to meet friends and relations and have fun. The most important festival was the **caribberie** *(kar RIB hur ee)*. The early European settlers called this festival a corroboree *(kuh ROB hur ee)*.

During a caribberie, the tribe acted out the events of the **Dreamtime** and of the tribe's history using music, songs, and dance. Men and women had separate roles to play in the event. Men often played the parts of animals and spirit beings while women sang and danced. The caribberie allowed everyone to connect to the Dreamtime. It was not a serious occasion, however. A caribberie was meant to be enjoyed. Everyone painted his or her body for the event, which lasted long into the night. Holding a caribberie was a common way for two tribes to make peace after a war.

▼ Aborigines perform a ritual dance in a painting made on a strip of tree bark. The bark was prepared for painting by being cleaned, smoothed, and flattened.

The caribberie was a public celebration. Anyone could attend. Many other ceremonies were restricted, and only people who had been initiated into adulthood and taught the secret **rituals** could attend. The longest ceremonies were funerals, which could last for weeks. It was important to show great respect to a dead person's spirit so that it was happy to go to the Land of the Dead. If a spirit was angry at its treatment, the Aborigines believed, it might stay behind and cause trouble for the living.

A Time for Trade

Trade meetings were another occasion to hold ceremonies. Aborigines needed to trade to get good stone for making tools; **ocher**, a soft mineral rich in iron, for body painting; and shells for body ornaments and magic charms. Aborigines did not use any form of money. They saw trade as an exchange of gifts. If someone was given a fine stone ax as a gift, he was expected to give a gift of equal value in return. Short ceremonies were held to mark the exchange. These gifts and ceremonies created a special relationship between the trading partners.

Exchanging gifts was a good way to keep in touch with distant relatives and to make friends with people in other tribes. A person who did not repay a gift would be ignored in the future. If the giver was angry, the recipient might even be cursed.

▼ Tree carvings were used to mark burial grounds. Carvers cut a piece of bark off the tree trunk, so that they could carve directly into the wood beneath. The carvings became partly hidden as the bark grew back, forming a long-lasting scar on the tree.

CEREMONIAL GROUNDS
In southeastern Australia, ceremonies were held in **sacred** places marked by circular earth or stone banks. Before a ceremony, Aborigines molded dirt into the shapes of spirit beings. Carvings on trees marked spots where funeral rituals and burials took place.

MUSIC, DANCE, AND STORYTELLING

The Aborigines had rich traditions of music, dance, song, and storytelling. These arts helped to teach people about the **Dreamtime** and about nature, history, and good behavior in an enjoyable way.

Everyone could join in and make music. Aboriginal musical instruments were simple to make and play. Musical instruments included clapping sticks, rattles made from seedpods, and drums made from hollow logs and animal skins. The most difficult Aboriginal instrument to play was the **didgeridoo** *(dihj uhr uh DOO)*. This wind instrument was made from a long, hollow branch. It made a steady, rhythmic, droning sound. Didgeridoos were originally used only in northern Australia. They are still used today and are popular with Aboriginal musicians all over Australia.

Singing was important to the Aborigines. They sang songs to bring luck in a hunt, to make rain, to make a child grow strong, and for many other reasons. The most important songs were those about the **songlines**, the tracks that the spirit beings made across the landscape during the Dreamtime. The

▼ A young Aborigine plays a wind instrument called a didgeridoo. His companions beat out a rhythm with clapping sticks.

GAMES FOR ADULTS AND CHILDREN

Aborigines played dozens of different games. Men and boys enjoyed games of skill involving throwing spears, clubs, and stones. A hide-and-seek game was popular with children. There were many ball games, including a rough form of football called marn grook. This game is believed to have inspired some of the rules of modern Australian Rules football.

spirits gave the Aborigines songs about these journeys. The songs described the landmarks along the way, how they were made, and how they got their names. The Aborigines could use the knowledge in these songs like maps to help them find their way on long journeys across country. Through songs about the songlines, people from different regions and **clans** could feel that they were linked to one another by a Dreamtime story about a traveling ancestral being. The song could have many parts, each dealing with a particular place and each in the care of particular people with some spiritual connection to that place.

▼ An Aborigine dances and plays clapping sticks in an ancient rock painting, from Faraway Bay in what is now the state of Western Australia. Clapping sticks are still used at Aboriginal dances.

Some dances also told stories. With paint decorating their bodies, dancers imitated the actions of wild animals and spirit beings. Men and women did not dance together. Children enjoyed dancing, but their dances were just for fun. They did not tell stories.

Secret Stories

Stories told around the campfire were the most important part of a child's education. They taught children their first lessons in tribal history, law, and religion. Not all stories were intended for everyone, however. Married women had stories they told only to one another. It was against tribal law for an unmarried girl to listen to them. There were also secret stories shared only by adult men. The **elders** were the keepers of the tribal stories. It was their duty to make sure that the stories were not lost or forgotten.

BODY PAINTING AND DRESS

Aborigines practiced body painting. They painted their bodies before such special occasions as **caribberies,** funerals, and initiation ceremonies, during which a child became an adult. Different designs were used to identify groups and tribes. For example, Aborigines in Arnhem Land in northern Australia painted their skin with bone patterns.

Aborigines used many different materials for body painting. Most body paints were made in the same way as the paints used for rock art. Aborigines also mixed **pigments** with vegetable oils. Sometimes people just smeared their bodies all over with red **ocher**. Aborigines also made patterns by cutting their skin. When the cuts healed, they left a permanent pattern of scars on the skin.

▲ A man applies paint to another in preparation for a special occasion. Different Aboriginal tribes could be identified by unique designs.

AN OCHER MINE

Ocher for body paint came from mines and quarries. One of the biggest mines was at Wilgie Mia in Western Australia. The Aborigines believed that the red ocher there had been created by the blood of a great kangaroo killed by the spirit Mondong. When people left the mine, they walked backward and swept away their footprints. They believed that this stopped Mondong from following and killing them, too.

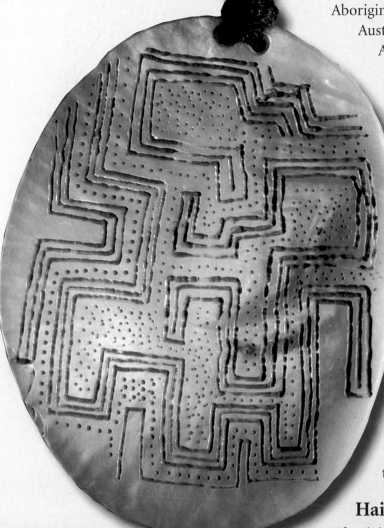

▲ A mother-of-pearl pendant with a string made of human hair. Aborigines valued mother-of-pearl because they associated its shiny surface with the Rainbow Snake, a **Dreamtime** being who brought rain. Some experts believe the design on the pendant represents the movement of water, clouds, and lightning.

Clothing

Aborigines rarely wore clothes. In southern Australia, where the weather is cooler, Aborigines wore capes made from kangaroo and opossum skins in winter. Usually, however, if Aborigines wanted to keep warm in winter, they carried slow-burning sticks called **firesticks** with them and held them close to their bodies. They were accustomed to sleeping outside without blankets, even on frosty nights, as long as they had a fire nearby. **Dingoes** also helped to keep them warm on cold nights.

Many Aborigines wore such ornaments as headbands and necklaces made of kangaroo teeth, shells, or rock crystals. Men carried painted-bark shields and spears decorated with carvings. The carvings often told stories from the tribe's history.

Hairstyles

Aborigines wore their hair in different styles. Some styles were unique to a single tribe. They were like an identity badge. Aborigines "cut" their hair by singeing it with burning sticks. Tasmanian Aborigines used a mixture of ash and ocher to mold their hair into braids. Other groups decorated their hair with leaves, feathers, and animal bones and teeth.

When the Aborigines first met Europeans in the 1700's, they were puzzled by the Europeans' clothes. Clothing made it hard for the Aborigines to tell the difference between men and women. Europeans were embarrassed by the Aborigines' nakedness and forced them to start wearing clothes.

Tools and Toolmaking

The Aborigines used only a few types of tools. All of their tools were made of stone, wood, bone, shell, or plant fibers. Aborigines had to move often and walk everywhere. Thus, their tools were usually lightweight and often had many functions. There was no point in owning more things than they could easily carry.

Aborigines, mostly males, made stone tools in two ways. They shaped tools like spearheads and knives by striking flakes off a stone using another stone as a hammer. This technique produced very sharp edges. The best stone for making this type of tool was flint, a hard and brittle mineral that flakes easily.

Tools like axes and adzes for woodworking were more complicated to make. First, the Aborigines made a rough edge on a stone by striking flakes off one side. Then they ground and polished the tool against another rough stone to create a smooth cutting edge. Volcanic rocks made the best axes. Workers fastened stone tools to wooden handles using a sticky gum made from tree sap. They also tied the stones to handles using string made of vegetable fibers. An important wooden tool was the **woomera**, a simple spear-throwing device.

▲ An Aboriginal knife, blade and handle, was fashioned from a piece of quartzite rock. The blade was sharpened by striking flakes off the stone using another stone as a hammer.

Bowls, Bags, and Digging Sticks

Sheets of bark were used to make a bowl called a **coolamon.** The bark was molded into a bowl shape by heating it over a fire. Rubbing the bowls with fat kept them in good condition. Women used coolamons to carry food, water, and even babies. They carried these bowls on their heads.

Aborigines also used a kind of container called a **dilly bag.** Women wove these string bags from fibers made from bark, grasses, or leaves. They used different colored fibers to create decorative patterns.

The digging stick was one of the Aboriginal woman's most important tools. Digging sticks, which were weighted with ring-shaped stones, were used to dig up roots for food. The extra weight helped drive the stick deeper into the ground.

▼ An Aborigine carves a bunduk (spear) from hard wood using traditional methods.

THE BOOMERANG

The **boomerang** *(BOO muh rang)* is a unique Aboriginal throwing stick used to hunt birds. Its curved and flattened shape helps the stick fly through the air like an airplane wing. A boomerang flies in a curve, which makes it hard for birds to guess where it is going and so get out of its path.

HUNTING

Aborigines hunted wild animals, gathered wild plants, fished, and collected shellfish. There were few places where food could be found year-round, so the Aborigines were **nomadic**. They moved camp often to find new sources of food. How often Aborigines moved depended on how **fertile** their territory was. In desert areas, a band of Aborigines might have to move almost every day to find food. In areas with more abundant plant and animal life, such as the south and east and along the coast, a band could stay in the same place for several months.

Aborigines had a strict division of labor. Hunting and fishing were men's work. Gathering shellfish and plants for food was women's work. Hunting trips might last several days, and they were not always successful. The favorite animals for hunting were kangaroos and **wallabies**. On the coast, Aborigines hunted seals. Hunters needed to be good trackers and have a detailed knowledge of animal behavior. They were experts at imitating the cries of wild animals and birds to attract them close enough to kill.

Men never talked to one another when hunting. They used touch and sign language to communicate without making a sound. When hunting, Aborigines smeared their bodies with soil to disguise their smell. They used spears to kill most animals but relied on **boomerangs** to kill birds.

▲ A hunter prepares to spear a kangaroo in a bark painting from Kakadu in northwestern Australia. The painting is done in the X-ray style, which shows the kangaroo's internal organs. The pattern of lines on such an image was particular to the tribe associated with the painting and was believed to give the figure spiritual power.

Gone Fishing

Aborigines caught fish using barbed spears, nets, and lines with hooks made from sea shells. They built circular stone walls in rivers. When river levels fell during the dry seasons, fish that were inside the stone walls were trapped and could easily be caught. Aborigines also placed long, narrow baskets of twigs in rivers to trap fish. The baskets were wide enough for fish to swim into. Once a fish was in the basket, however, there was no room for it to turn around, so it could not escape.

▼ An Aborigine hunts in a swamp in the traditional manner. In his right hand, the hunter holds a spear notched into a **woomera,** a simple device that increased the distance that a spear could be thrown. In his left hand, he carries a spare spear and a boomerang. A stone ax hangs at his waist.

HOW TO CATCH AN EMU

An **emu** (EE myoo) is a large ostrich-like, flightless bird. Emus can run as fast as 35 miles (55 kilometers) per hour and are impossible to catch on foot. They are extremely curious, however. If a hunter imitated the movement of an emu with a stick and bunch of feathers, an emu might come to him to investigate. Death awaited the curious emu. The hunter would disable the emu by hitting it with a large stone or a boomerang, and then kill it with a spear.

GATHERING FOOD

▲ Aborigines ate a wide range of wild plant foods that Australian settlers called "bush tucker." These foods include dark blue wild plums, bright red riberries, and many different seeds and nuts. They are laid out on soft paper-bark, which was used to wrap food.

Everyone was pleased when the men returned with meat from a successful hunting trip. Meat was regarded as the best food. The women, however, provided most of the Aborigines' food.

Aborigines ate dozens of kinds of grass seeds, roots, fruits, and nuts. Many plant foods needed careful preparation before they could be eaten. The fern-like **cycad** *(SY kad)* has nutritious buds but contains poisons that had to be washed or cooked out. Wild **yams** were baked in ash to destroy the poisons they contain. Grass and water lily seeds were ground to make flour. The flour was mixed with water to make flat cakes.

A woman's most important tools were a digging stick to dig up roots and a **coolamon** to carry food back to the camp. Usually it took the women only a few hours to gather enough food to feed everyone in the group. At certain times of the year, however, food would become scarce. In the desert, this time was the hot summer. In the cooler south, winter was the hard time. The Aborigines dried fruit and sometimes buried stores of seeds, yams, and cycads for use in emergencies. However, they could not build up large stores of food because they could not carry them when they moved camp.

In coastal areas, women collected shellfish from rock pools and dug clams from sandy beaches. In Tasmania, women went diving in the ocean for abalone *(ab uh LOH nee)*, a type of snail prized for its meat. In rivers and lakes, women collected freshwater mussels and crayfish.

Aboriginal Cooking

Aborigines had no cooking pots and could not boil water. Aboriginal cooking was, therefore, very simple. They roasted meat on a fire. Usually Aborigines preferred to eat their meat only lightly cooked. They used hot stones as griddles to cook seed cakes. Vegetables and bird eggs were buried in hot ashes and baked. Some Aborigines used clay ovens for cooking.

INSECT FOODS

Aborigines also ate protein-rich insects. A favorite was the juicy witchetty *(WIHCH uh tee)* grub (below), which lives in rotting wood. The grubs are said to taste like eggs, and Aborigines usually ate them raw.

GROWING UP

Children in Aboriginal societies grew up faster than children in modern societies. Mothers nursed their babies until the children were old enough to eat the same foods as adults, usually when they were about 3 years old. Until children were old enough to walk, they spent all their time with their mothers. Mothers carried infants in **coolamons** lined with soft bark and leaves.

Children were allowed great freedom, and their parents rarely punished them for behaving badly. Children learned the skills they would need as adults by working alongside their parents. Girls

▼ Aborigine boys practice throwing a **boomerang**. Children were not closely supervised by their parents and were free to roam.

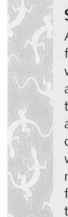

SIMPLE TOYS
Aborigine children had few toys. They played with balls made from animal hide, spinning tops, and models of adult tools like axes and canoes. Girls played with wooden dolls and made rings and hoops from grass and leaves to wear as ornaments.

went out looking for food plants with their mothers. They learned which plants could be eaten and how to prepare them by watching and asking questions. They were given their own little collecting bags and digging sticks so that they could help gather food.

Boys were not allowed to go on hunting trips with the men until they became teenagers. Until then, they were free to roam in groups. They hunted small animals by themselves or practiced lighting fires. Boys and girls had plenty of time to play together. In some areas, there were special children's songs. Chanting the songs helped the children learn the names of animals and plants and other things they needed to know in everyday life. There were no schools, but adults—often their grandparents—taught children about Aboriginal religious beliefs and history by telling them stories.

Ceremonies for Becoming an Adult

Both boys and girls had to take part in special ceremonies before they could officially become adults. The ceremonies took place when children were between the ages of 10 and 14. During the ceremonies, adults taught the children information that had been kept secret during their childhood. Adulthood ceremonies were simpler for girls than for boys, and after such a ceremony, a girl was considered ready for marriage. During initiation ceremonies, boys could be scarred or have their teeth knocked out. These painful **rituals** left permanent marks but allowed everyone to see that a boy had become a man.

▶ A father prepares his son for his adulthood initiation ceremony. The boy's body has been painted with symbols believed to have been given to his clan in the **Dreamtime** by the spirit beings.

HEALTH AND MEDICINES

Aborigines believed that illnesses were caused by harmful magic. Aboriginal healers used both magic and medicine to treat illnesses. Medicine could make the patient feel more comfortable, but magic was needed to break the spell that they believed caused the illness.

The Aborigines had a detailed knowledge of **medicinal** plants. They used over 100 different plants to treat a wide range of illnesses. One of the most useful was the eucalyptus *(yoo kuh LIHP tuhs)* tree. It is rich in a strong-smelling oil that can be extracted by soaking its bark or leaves in water. This liquid was used for treating colds, headaches, and strained muscles. Eucalyptus oil is so beneficial that many modern medicines use it.

Another very useful plant was the acacia *(uh KAY shuh)* tree. The gum that oozes from acacia bark can be used to treat diarrhea. It can also kill **parasites** that live in the intestines. Aborigines soaked acacia bark in water to make a treatment for sore throats and coughs. They also made a powerful drug from

◀ Eucalyptus trees are rich in a strong-smelling oil that Aborigines used to treat headaches, muscle pains, and colds. Eucalyptus is still used to treat many ailments.

SURVIVING SURGERY

Aborigines sometimes performed simple surgery. A European explorer described the treatment of a man whose stomach had been split open so that his intestines had fallen out. After the wounded man was given water to drink, the healer watched to see if his intestines leaked. If they did, it meant that the wounded man would soon die. There was no leak, so the healer gently washed the man's intestines and pushed them back inside. The healer then treated the wound with medicinal herbs, sealed it with clay, and bandaged it with bark. This man made a quick recovery. Aboriginal surgery did not always work, however.

the leaves of the pituri *(PIHCH uh ree)* plant. When they chewed this drug in small amounts, it cured tiredness. In large amounts, however, pituri was poisonous. The Aborigines threw it into ponds to stun fish and make them easier to catch.

Tooth Troubles

The Aborigines had little sugar in their diet so they did not suffer from tooth decay. Eating tough, gritty foods like roots eventually wore their teeth down to the nerves, however. The Aborigines used shredded wood from the green plum tree to cure toothaches.

▶ A burst of yellow flowers adorns an Australian acacia, also called a wattle. Aborigines used medicines made from the bark and gum of acacia trees to treat many illnesses.

PEOPLE OF THE COAST

The southeast coast of Australia was a favorable place for Aborigines to live. They could hunt game and collect plant foods in the coastal forests. Swamps and marshes around river **estuaries** *(EHS chu EHR eez)* were good places to trap water birds and turtles and to collect edible water plants. The sea provided a variety of food all year round. The region has a pleasant climate, with good rainfall, warm summers, and mild winters with little frost or snow.

Aborigines camped on high headlands from which they could watch the movement of birds and animals along the coast. Natural rock shelters and caves in sea cliffs also made good campsites. Aborigines returned to the same campsites year after year. If food was plentiful, the Aborigines could stay at the same campsite for several months and rarely needed to travel far inland. **Archaeologists** can identify campsites from the large mounds of discarded shells, bones, ash, and broken tools that built up over the years. Wide flat stones are found at many campsites. These were heated on fires and used as griddles to cook fish. The Aborigines also carved pictures of people, fish, whales, and land animals on rocks. These pictures often marked the places where boys were initiated into adulthood.

▼ Wallabies (below) and kangaroos resemble each other, but wallabies are generally smaller. Aborigines living along Australia's southeast coast hunted wallabies and other game and generally had plentiful supplies of meat.

The coastal Aborigines fished from bark canoes or rocks on the shore using nets, three-pronged spears called tridents *(TRY duhntz)*, and hooks and lines. Only men used nets and spears, but both men and women fished with hooks and lines. The Aborigines made fishing hooks from mother-of-pearl. The smooth, shiny surface of mother-of-pearl reflects light. The flashes of light attracted fish to the hooks, so they did not need to be baited. Women also collected mussels from rocky shores.

Plentiful Supplies of Meat

Men hunted for kangaroos, **wallabies**, and opossums inland, and they hunted along the coast for seals, penguins, and other sea birds. The meat from one seal would feed a band of Aborigines for several days. The Aborigines killed stranded whales, but they lacked boats that were strong and fast enough to hunt whales at sea. Aborigines valued seals, whales, and other sea **mammals** for their plentiful fat. Most wild animals have little body fat. Aborigines thus usually found it hard to get enough fat in their diet. Thanks to the wide range of foods available, the Aborigines of the southeast coast were among the healthiest and best-nourished people in Australia.

THE NUT FESTIVAL

In January and February, the Aborigines who lived near the south-central coast (in what is now the state of Queensland) feasted on the nuts of bunya pine trees (below). Every three years the pines had an extra-large crop of nuts. When this happened, groups from neighboring areas were invited to take part in the harvest because there were more than enough nuts for everyone. This turned the harvest into a festival, with singing, dancing, and socializing. Giant, 8-inch- (20-centimeter-) long pine cones contain the nutritious and tasty nuts. Falling cones sometimes injured, or even killed, unwary harvesters on the ground below. Fortunately, the cones made a whistling sound as they fell, which served as a warning to harvesters to get out of the way.

PEOPLE OF THE DESERT

Australia is the world's most **arid** continent. About one-third of Australia is desert, and much of the rest is dry grassland with scattered shrubs and trees. Thanks to their detailed knowledge of their environment, Aborigines were able to live in even these harsh places.

The Aborigines who lived in the deserts were true **nomads**. Because water is scarce in deserts, so is food. Each band needed a territory covering hundreds of square miles. The food within easy reach of a campsite was quickly used up. Every few days, the band had to move on. The most plentiful food in the desert was wild grass seeds.

The Search for Water

The desert Aborigines were skilled at finding water. They needed to remember the exact location of wells in a landscape with few natural features. They covered wells with stones to stop animals from dirtying the water. If the wells dried up, Aborigines got water by watching the flights of birds and the paths of marching ants. They knew that these animals could lead them to hidden pools of water trapped in the hollows of tree trunks.

Aborigines also collected the dew that formed on desert plants. Desert nights are cold because the land quickly loses the heat it absorbs during the day. Because cooler night air holds less moisture than warmer daytime air, some

▼ A rock shelter in Western Australia. Such shelters shaded Aborigines from the scorching sun.

of the moisture collects as water droplets on cool surfaces. By morning, the grass is usually wet with dew. By brushing this dew into containers, Aborigines could collect up to 2 pints (1 liter) of water in an hour.

Some trees have hollow roots that contain water. Aborigines dug these up and chopped them open. They were careful not to take so much water that the tree would die, because eventually they might need to collect water from the tree again.

At certain times of the year, bands from a wide area gathered at reliable water holes to hold religious festivals. Festivals were also opportunities to make friends and find marriage partners from other **clans.** These friendships and family links helped the Aborigines survive. In an unusually dry year, a band might have to abandon its own territory. If they had friends and family with another band, they would be allowed to move into its territory until food became more plentiful.

▲ Zebra finches, named for their black and white striped plumage, drink from pools of water that form between the branches of trees. Aborigines learned to find these hidden water sources by carefully following the movements of the finches.

SEASONS OF THE DESERT YEAR

Aborigines recognized from three to six seasons in a year, depending on where they lived. The Anangu Aborigines who lived in the deserts of central Australia recognized five seasons: Piryakatu (August to October)—the breeding season for animals; Mai Wiyaringkupai (November to December)—the hot summer season when food becomes scarce; Itjanu (January to March)—the rainy season; Wanitjunkupai (April to May)—the cool, cloudy season; and Wari (June to July)—the cold winter season with frosty nights. Different Aboriginal groups had different names for the seasons.

PEOPLE OF THE RIVERS

The most densely populated part of Australia before the arrival of European settlers was the Murray River Valley in southeastern Australia. Because this area had an ample water supply, it was rich in game. There were so many different sources of food that the Aborigines who lived in this area were able to live in one place for most of the year.

The Murray River flows through dry country. Many kinds of wildlife come to drink at the river. The river is rich in fish, and dozens of **species** of food plants grow along its wooded banks. The Aborigines used nets that were up to 100 yards (90 meters) long to catch fish and wildfowl on the river. They also used the nets on land to trap kangaroos and **emus**. The women collected crayfish and freshwater mussels from the river and seeds and **yams** along the riverbanks. In the spring, the men raided the nests of geese to collect their eggs.

▲ In an Aborigine camp on the Murray River, men make tools of stone and wood and craft a bark canoe. Women prepare and cook food, such as wild plants and fish speared in the river. One of the women carries food in a **coolamon**. The group may be expecting trouble from a neighboring **clan,** as a warrior stands guard with shield and spear.

To help with fishing and travel along the river, the Aborigines made canoes from sheets of bark. Both adults and children liked to relax on the riverbank and swim or play in shallow water.

A Year on the River

These Aborigines did not have to move camp often, and they rarely traveled far from the riverbank. Food was most plentiful in the spring, the wettest time of year. Rain and melted snow from nearby mountains caused the river to overflow and flood the surrounding countryside. Mud left behind by the floods kept the land **fertile**. By fall, the land was drying out. Little rain fell in winter so food was always short at that time of year.

The Aborigines could live well most of the time. But if there was a **drought** *(drowt)*, a long period with little or no rainfall, the Murray began to dry up. When this happened, the fish disappeared and the wildfowl left. The Aborigines starved.

Moth Feast

The Koori people left the Murray River in summer to catch bogong *(BOH gawng)* moths in the Australian Alps. Millions of moths sheltered from the heat under rocks and were easily caught. After their legs and wings had been pulled off, the moths were roasted and then pounded into cakes.

▼ The Murray cod is Australia's largest freshwater fish, growing to well over 3 feet (1 meter) long. This type of fish was an important food for Aborigines living along the Murray River. After the arrival of Europeans, the number of Murray cod declined because of overfishing.

THE TASMANIANS

▲ The interior of Tasmania is mountainous and densely forested and has a climate that is often cold and wet. Most Tasmanian Aborigines lived close to the coast.

The Tasmanians *(taz MAY nee uhnz)* were among the most isolated people in the world. During the last **ice age**, a land bridge linked Tasmania to the Australian mainland. When the last ice age ended, sea levels rose, and about 8,000 years ago, Tasmania became an island. From that time until the arrival of the French explorer Marion du Fresne *(doo frehn)* in 1772, the Tasmanians had no contact with any other people.

The Tasmanians remained isolated for such a long time because neither they nor the mainland Aborigines could make seaworthy boats. The Tasmanians made their boats by tying together bundles of reeds and bark. These boats could make short journeys on rivers or along the coast, but they were not strong enough for long sea journeys. The Tasmanian Aborigines shared many cultural practices with the Aborigines on the mainland. However, because they became isolated, they developed in unique ways as well.

According to some estimates, there were only about 3,000 Tasmanians at any one time. Tasmania had fewer edible plants and less wildlife than the mainland, so the island could not support a large population. The Tasmanians lived in bands of up to 80 people scattered along the coast. The most important source of food for the Tasmanians was shellfish. The Tasmanians also hunted seals and seabirds along the coast and **wallabies** and other small animals inland. They collected fungi and plant foods in the forests. The early Tasmanians ate a great deal of fish. However, the Tasmanians abandoned fishing at some point in the distant past, though **archaeologists** are unsure why.

The Simplest Tool Kit

At the time that Europeans arrived, the Tasmanians used only about two dozen different objects. Archaeologists believe that the Tasmanians had one of the most basic tool kits of any living population. Tools that were common on the mainland, such as **boomerangs** and fishing nets, were unknown to the Tasmanians. New technology did not reach Tasmania. The Tasmanians did not invent new technology themselves because there were so few of them, and inventors are rare in any community. Experts believe that the Tasmanians lost the skill of making fire. They always carried slow-burning

▲ A Tasmanian Aboriginal rock carving shows an abalone shell. Tasmanian women collected abalones by diving along the rocky coast. Abalones were plentiful and were prized for their tasty meat.

branches, called **firesticks**, with them to light fires. If their fire went out, they had to wait until lightning started a natural bush fire to collect new firesticks or else get firesticks from a neighboring band.

European settlers established a settlement on Tasmania in 1803. Conflict soon broke out between the colonists and the Aborigines, and many of the Aborigines were killed. The colonists forced the remaining Tasmanian Aborigines to live on a small island north of the main island, where many more died of disease and starvation. Less than 5 percent of Tasmanians today claim to be descended from Aborigines.

THE LAST TASMANIAN?

The last Tasmanian of pure Aborigine descent may have been a woman named Truganini *(troo guh NEE nee)* (1812-1876). After her death, the Tasmanian Museum and Art Gallery in Hobart displayed her skeleton for many years. Her bones were finally returned to the Aborigine community in 1976. Her remains were cremated and scattered in the sea. Some evidence indicates there may have been other tribal Tasmanian Aborigines who outlived her, however.

THE TORRES STRAIT ISLANDERS

The Torres Strait Islanders live on islands in the sea between northern Australia and New Guinea. Although the islanders probably descended from the same people as the Aborigines, the islanders had a different way of life from the Aborigines. Torres Straits Islanders consider themselves to be a separate people from the Aborigines.

Seafarers from New Guinea probably settled the islands more than 50,000 years ago. The islands are small and have little game for hunting. The islanders relied on fishing, collecting shellfish, and hunting sea turtles and large sea **mammals** called dugongs *(DOO gongz)*. The islanders also grew such food plants as **yams** and raised pigs, both of which the earliest settlers probably brought from New Guinea.

▼ Seafarers from New Guinea settled Murray Island (below) and other islands in the Torres Strait more than 50,000 years ago. Although the first islanders were probably descended from the same people as the Aborigines of Australia, the Torres Strait Islanders consider themselves to be a separate people.

THE OUTRIGGER CANOE

For fishing and trade, the islanders used outrigger canoes. This type of canoe is widespread in the Indian and Pacific oceans. Outriggers are wooden floats fastened on the ends of poles extending from the sides of the canoe. Outriggers were excellent for long ocean voyages because the floats prevent the canoe from turning over in rough seas. The islanders paddled the canoes and sometimes used a sail.

The people of each island were independent. They were divided into family groups and chose leaders only in times of war. The islanders were headhunters. Taking the head of an enemy was a way for a boy to become a man. In addition, heads were valuable trade items.

Unlike the Australian Aborigines, the islanders did not believe in the **Dreamtime**. Instead, they believed that ancient heroes created the world. Magic played a large part in the Torres Islanders' spiritual beliefs, as it did for the Australian Aborigines. Dance and **ritual** were also important. One of the islanders' most important rituals was a funeral ceremony called the tombstone opening. This ceremony incorporated feasting and dancing to celebrate the life of someone who had recently died.

Traders

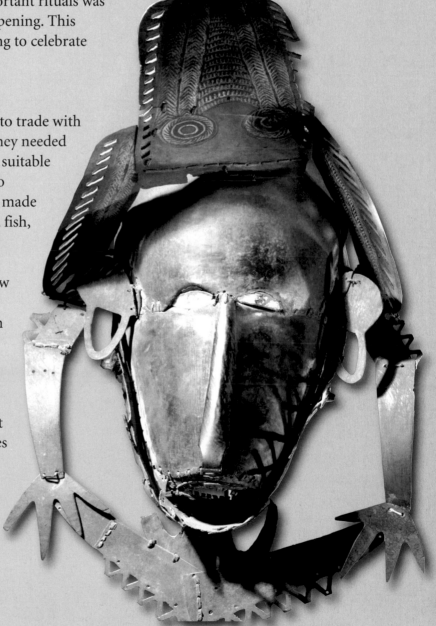

The people of the Torres Strait Islands had to trade with other peoples to get many of the supplies they needed for daily life. The islands did not have trees suitable for making their own canoes, so they had to exchange items from the islands for canoes made in New Guinea. These items included dried fish, sea turtles, harpoons and ornaments made of mother-of-pearl, and even women. The islanders also obtained some food from New Guinea, such as sago *(SAY goh)*, a starch found in the spongy center of tropical palm trees. Other items imported from New Guinea included drums, stone clubs, bows and arrows, and exotic bird feathers. With the Aborigines, the islanders traded for spears and **ocher**. At times, the Torres Strait Islanders acted as a link between the peoples of Australia and New Guinea, because they were in contact with both groups.

▶ A dance mask from the Torres Strait Islands is made of pieces of tortoise shell sewn together with thread made from palm tree fibers. The mask was imported to the islands from New Guinea.

THE COMING OF THE EUROPEANS

The Dutch were the first Europeans to reach Australia. In 1606, Captain Willem Jansz landed on the northern coast. He quickly left after the local Aborigines killed some of his crewmembers. Over the next few years, other Dutch captains gradually explored the northern, western, and southern coasts of Australia. In 1642, the Dutch explorer Abel Tasman reached the island now known as Tasmania.

Tasman named the continent New Holland after his homeland. The British later renamed it Australia, meaning *southern land*. The Dutch, who were primarily looking for such trade goods as spices and precious metals, soon lost interest in the region. The parts of Australia they had explored were barren, and they did not try to settle the land.

Great Britain Claims Australia

In 1770, British Captain James Cook explored the eastern coast of Australia. Unlike the coasts the Dutch had explored, this coast was green and **fertile**. Cook thought that it looked like a good place to start a settlement and claimed Australia for Great Britain.

▼ Dutch sea captains explored the northern, western, and southern coasts of Australia in the 1600's. In 1770, British Captain James Cook, who sailed along the more fertile eastern coast, claimed Australia for Britain.

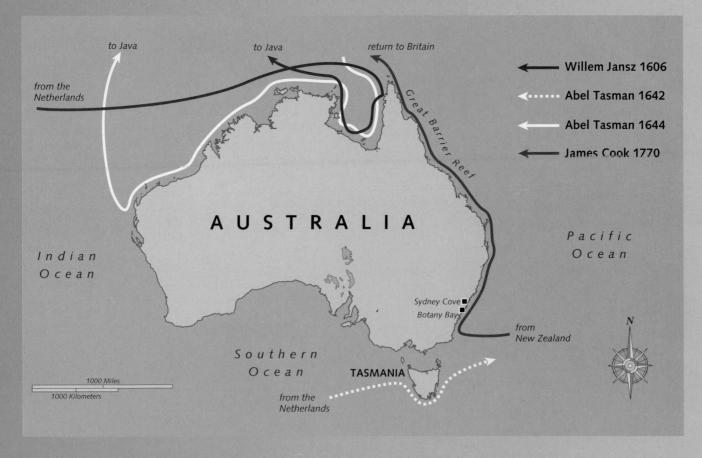

to Java

to Java

return to Britain

from the Netherlands

Willem Jansz 1606

Abel Tasman 1642

Abel Tasman 1644

James Cook 1770

Great Barrier Reef

AUSTRALIA

Indian Ocean

Pacific Ocean

Sydney Cove
Botany Bay

from New Zealand

1000 Miles

1000 Kilometers

Southern Ocean

TASMANIA

from the Netherlands

N

JAMES COOK
(1728-1779)

The British sailor James Cook (shown here in a portrait painted by Nathaniel Dance Holland) is considered one of the greatest explorers of the 1700's. From 1768 to 1771, 1772 to 1775, and 1776 to 1779, Cook led three voyages to explore the Pacific Ocean. During the first of these voyages, Cook became the first European to explore the east coast of Australia, and he claimed Australia for Great Britain. In 1778, Cook became the first European to visit Hawaii. He was killed there in a fight with the islanders in 1779.

In 1787, the British government began punishing criminals by "transporting" them, that is, sending them to Australia for the rest of their lives. Officials believed that this would be cheaper than keeping them in prison in Great Britain. Australia was so far away that there would also be little chance that the prisoners would escape and return home. In January 1788, the first party of about 750 convicts arrived at Botany Bay, on Australia's east coast. A few days later they began to establish a **penal colony** nearby, after the fleet was moved north to a better harbor, which was named Sydney Cove.

ABORIGINAL RESISTANCE

British colonists did not respect the Aborigines' way of life. They saw the Aborigines as "savages" who were no better than animals. The British thought that the Aborigines were too primitive to understand the idea of land ownership. They acted as if Australia were *terra nullius*, which means *no one's land* in Latin. Although early governors were officially instructed to obtain the Aborigines' consent before Europeans settled on Aboriginal land, the British authorities did not negotiate with the Aborigines. British officials granted land to settlers and nearly always forgave settlers who just seized whatever they wanted.

Sometimes, Aborigines tried to resist the settlers by burning their crops and killing their livestock. The settlers attacked the Aborigines in revenge, killing men, women, and children. The settlers' guns and horses gave them a great advantage over the Aborigines, who were on foot and armed only with spears. The Aborigines knew the land well, however, and were experts at moving silently

AN ABORIGINE RESISTANCE FIGHTER

Pemulwuy *(PEHM uhl wee)* led the Eora Aborigine people in their struggle against the first British settlers. He was defeated and captured at the battle of Parramatta in 1797. Despite being wounded, he escaped from prison. Pemulwuy claimed he did this by turning himself into a bird. Pemulwuy was killed in 1802.

◀ Captain James Cook raises the British flag at Botany Bay and claims Australia for Great Britain on August 22, 1770, in a painting by Algernon Talmage. The British refused to accept the Aborigines' claims to the land.

and hiding in the bush. About 3,000 troops sent to round up Aborigines in Tasmania in 1830 managed to capture only 2 people. Attacks on the Aborigines continued, in some remote regions, until as recently as 1928.

The Effect of Diseases

The settlers accidentally introduced many diseases to Australia, including smallpox, influenza *(ihn flu EHN zuh)*, measles, and typhoid *(TY foyd)*. **Epidemics** *(ehp uh DEHM ihkz)*, or widespread outbreaks, of these diseases probably killed far more Aborigines than were estimated to have been killed in wars with the settlers.

Aborigines also faced starvation because the settlers hunted the game that they depended on for food. Some regions lost their entire Aboriginal populations.

▲ Aborigines and white Australian supporters display the Aboriginal flag in a land-rights protest in the city of Sydney. The flag became an official national flag of Australia in 1995.

Aborigines whose land was invaded by settlers could either move into the territory of another tribe or become the servants of the settlers. Sometimes wars broke out among the Aborigines when tribes tried to defend their territories against trespassers. In many cases, Aborigines tried to stay in their own territory and reach some kind of accommodation with the settlers.

By 1921, wars, disease, and starvation had reduced the number of Aborigines to only about 62,000. In Tasmania, tribal Aborigines had probably been completely wiped out by the early 1900's, though some people of mixed Aboriginal-European descent survived.

THE ABORIGINES TODAY

The settlers' violent attacks on the Aborigines ended in the 1920's, though violent treatment by police and employers continued unpunished for many years. Even after the 1920's, white Australians often forced Aborigines to live on government reservations and took away their children to be raised like white Australians. They intended to destroy Aboriginal culture.

The loss of their lands made it impossible for the Aborigines to continue their traditional way of life. In some remote areas, Aborigines did not lose their land, though they came under European supervision. In regions remote from the major cities, about one-quarter of the Aboriginal population today lives on land that it owns. Many of these Aborigines depend on government aid. They also sell artworks and craft items and hunt meat and collect wild plant foods. No Aborigines now depend entirely on hunting and gathering for a living, however.

Aborigines have adopted many of the ways of white Australians. Aborigines use such modern technology as guns, automobiles, and motorboats. They watch television and dress in the same style of clothing as white Australians. Many Aborigines have become Christians. Often Christian beliefs are mixed with a continuing belief in the **Dreamtime**. Many Aborigines have lost their traditional languages and now speak only English. However, Aboriginal languages are still widely spoken in the north and the central deserts.

Many Aborigines make a living in the same way as white Australians, for example, as farmhands and laborers, teachers, and doctors. Some Aborigines

▲ Modern Aboriginal art, including this painting by Turkey Tolson Tjupurrula (above), is often based on traditional patterns. Tjupurrula lived all of his life on his **clan's** ancestral lands in Australia's Northern Territory. Until he reached his late teens, Tjupurrula lived the traditional life of a **nomadic** Aborigine hunter-gatherer.

still practice traditional crafts, mainly to produce objects for the tourist market. Paintings by modern Aboriginal artists are popular with collectors.

Unfortunately, Aborigines still face racial prejudice. They are much more likely to be unemployed and to depend on government aid than white Australians.

Aboriginal Rights Campaign

During the 1960's, Aborigines began to campaign for their political and land rights. In 1962, Aborigines were finally allowed to vote in national elections, and they gained other privileges of Australian citizenship in a series of legal reforms from the 1940's to the 1970's. Between 1966 and 1993, the state and national governments of Australia gave Aborigines the right to try to establish ownership to the land that had not yet been taken from them by settlers. Australians and their governments have gradually come to accept that the Aborigines owned Australia before Europeans arrived, but most of Australia remains under non-Aboriginal ownership. About 20 percent of Australia is now owned by Aborigines, and more is being purchased for them by the national government each year. However, it is not easy to make this land profitable, and Aborigines still face a struggle to achieve full equality with white Australians. Only in 2008 did the Australian government officially apologize to the Aborigines for separating Aboriginal children from their families.

WHITE AUSTRALIA APOLOGIZES

Speaking at Australia's Parliament House on Feb. 13, 2008, Prime Minister Kevin Rudd apologized to the Aborigines for the wrongs done to them by white Australians. "For the indignity and degradation thus inflicted on a proud people and a proud culture, we say sorry." Outdoor screens were set up around the country to allow people to view the speech live. Many Aborigines welcomed the apology, but others complained that Rudd should also have offered compensation.

GLOSSARY

anthropologist A scientist who studies humanity and human culture.

archaeologist A scientist who studies the remains of past human cultures.

archaeology The scientific study of the remains of past human cultures.

arid Dry.

australite A small, button- or lens-shaped piece of glass found in southern Australia probably formed by the impact of a meteorite and shaped by a rapid flight through the atmosphere. Known elsewhere as a tektite.

billabong A pool or small lake left behind when a river changes course.

boomerang An Aboriginal throwing stick used as a weapon.

caribberie An important Aboriginal festival. Called a corroboree by Australian settlers.

carnivore An animal that eats meat.

clan A group of people who are related through a common ancestor.

coolamon An elongated bark bowl used mainly by Aboriginal women.

cycad A large palmlike plant.

didgeridoo A musical instrument made from a straight, hollowed-out piece of wood that the Aborigines of northern Australia play in their religious ceremonies.

dilly bag A woven bag made from bark, grass, or leaves.

dingo A wild dog of Australia.

Dreamings Spirit beings who shaped the land during the **Dreamtime**.

Dreamtime The age (also called the Dreaming) when spirits called **Dreamings** created the landscape, plants, animals, and human beings.

drought A long period of dry weather.

dung The solid waste left by an animal after digesting food; when dried, dung can be burned as a fuel.

elder An older and more influential member of a tribe or community.

emu A large flightless bird similar to an ostrich.

epidemic A widespread outbreak of a disease.

estuary A broad mouth of a river, into which the tide flows.

excavate To uncover or unearth by digging, especially used of archaeological sites.

extinct Died out completely.

fertile Able to easily produce crops (when used about land or soil).

firestick A slow-burning branch used for warmth or to light fires.

ice age A period in Earth's history when ice sheets cover vast regions of land.

kaolin A fine white clay.

mammal The class of animals that feed their young on the mother's milk.

manganese A brittle, silver-gray metallic element.

marsupial A group of **mammals** whose young are born in an extremely immature state. Female marsupials usually have a pouch to protect their babies.

medicinal Useful as medicine.

megafauna Large animals.

nomadic Moving from place to place in search of food.

ocher Any one of various earthy mixtures containing clay and iron oxide, ranging in coloring from pale yellow to orange, brown, and red, used as **pigments.**

parasite An animal or plant that lives on or in another from which it gets its food, always at the expense of the host.

penal colony A settlement outside a country where the country sends its prisoners.

pigment A coloring matter, especially a powder or some easily pulverized dry substance. Paint and dyes are made by mixing pigments with oil, water, or some other liquid.

ritual A solemn or important act or ceremony, often religious in nature.

sacred Holy.

shell mound Large piles of discarded shells, animal bones, and ash built up over hundreds of years.

songlines Tracks left on the landscape by the spirit beings during the **Dreamtime.**

species A type of animal or plant.

Uluru A giant outcrop of rock, also known as Ayers Rock, in the Northern Territory of Australia that is a place of spiritual significance for its traditional owners, the Anangu people, an Australian Aboriginal group.

wallaby A common species of **marsupial,** related to the kangaroo.

woomera A device used to throw spears.

yam A starchy root similar to a sweet potato. Yams are an important type of food in tropical areas.

ADDITIONAL RESOURCES

BOOKS

Aboriginal Art and Culture
by Jane Bingham (Raintree, 2005)

Aboriginal Art of Australia
by Carol Finley (Lerner, 1999)

Aboriginal Australians
by Diana Marshall (Weigl, 2004)

The Aboriginal Peoples of Australia
by Anne Bartlett (Lerner, 2002)

Australian Aborigines
by Steven Ferry (Smart Apple Media, 1999)

Dreamtime: Aboriginal Stories
by Oodgeroo Noonuccal (Lothrop, Lee & Shepard, 1994)

WEB SITES

http://www.dreamtime.net.au/index.cfm

http://library.thinkquest.org/C005462/indexto.html

INDEX

Acknowledgments

Alamy: 29 (Vikki Martin), 46 (Gondwana Photo Art), 49 (Bill Bachman), 51 (Bruce Miller); **The Art Archive:** 19 (Culver Pictures), 28 (Musée des Arts Africains et Océaniens/Alfredo Dagli Orti), 45 (Global Book Publishing), 55 (Harper Collins Publishers), 56 (Eileen Tweedy); **Bridgeman Art Library:** 18 (The Stapleton Collection); **Corbis:** 4 (Patrick Ward), 5 (Robert Francis/Robert Harding World Imagery), 7 (DK Limited), 8 (Michael Amendolia), 9, 22, 31 (Barry Lewis), 11 (image100), 12 (Dave G. Houser), 14 (Eric and David Hosking), 15 (Jack Fields), 16 (Joe Castro/epa), 21 (Chris Rainier), 23 (O. Alamany and E. Vicens), 25 (Steve Kaufman), 27 (Ralph A. Clevenger), 30, 35, 40, 41 (Penny Tweedie), 32 (Craig Lamotte), 34, 38 (Oliver Strewe), 37 (Steve Bowman), 39 (Claire Leimbach/Robert Harding World Imagery), 42 (Theo Allofs/zefa), 44 (Moodboard), 47 (Chris Boydell/Australian Picture Library), 52 (Ludo Kuipers), 57 (Tim Graham), 58 (Frans Lanting), 59 (Andrea Hayward/epa); **Getty Images:** 13 (National Geographic); **The Kobal Collection:** 26 (Fandango Australia); **PCL/Alamy:** 17; **Shutterstock:** 20 (Kaspars Grinvalds), 43, 50; **Werner Forman Archive:** 1, 33 (Tara Collection, New York), 24 (no photographer credited), 36 (private collection, Prague), 53 (Entwistle Gallery, London).

Cover image: **The Art Archive** (Dagli Orti/Musée des Arts Africains et Océaniens)
Back cover image: **Shutterstock** (Joop Snijder, Jr.)